P9-CRF-527

TOP 10

PARENTS KEEP OUT!

Nature

A FIREFLY BOOK

Published by Firefly Books Ltd. 2015

Copyright © 2015 Octopus Publishing Group Ltd

All rights reserved. No part of this publication may be reproduced, stored in a retrieval system, or transmitted in any form or by any means, electronic, mechanical, photocopying, recording or otherwise, without the prior written permission of the Publisher.

First printing

Publisher Cataloging-in-Publication Data (U.S.)

Terry, Paul, 1978-
    Top 10 for kids : nature / Paul Terry.
[96] pages : color illustrations ; cm.
Summary: "A weird and wonderful book full of checklists for kids, displaying fun facts and answers questions such as: where is Earth's biggest volcano and what's the tallest tree on the planet" - Provided by publisher.
ISBN-13: 978-1-77085-563-2 (pbk.)
1. Earth (Planet) - Miscellanea - Juvenile literature. I. Title. II. Top ten for kids : nature.
550 dc23   QB638.T4669 2015

Library and Archives Canada Cataloguing in Publication

Terry, Paul, 1978-, author
        Top 10 for kids : awesome earth / Paul Terry.
ISBN 978-1-77085-563-2 (pbk.)
        1. Earth (Planet)-Miscellanea-Juvenile literature. I. Title.
II. Title: Top ten for kids.
QB638.T47 2015   j550   C2015-902938-4

Published in the United States by
Firefly Books (U.S.) Inc.
P.O. Box 1338, Ellicott Station
Buffalo, New York 14205

Published in Canada by
Firefly Books Ltd.
50 Staples Avenue, Unit 1
Richmond Hill, Ontario L4B 0A7

Printed in China

First published in Great Britain in 2015 by Ticktock,
an imprint of Octopus Publishing Group Ltd
Carmelite House
50 Victoria Embankment
London, EC4Y 0DZ
Written by: Paul Terry. Paul Terry asserts the moral
right to be identified as the author of this work.
Series Editor/Project Editor: Anna Bowles
Managing Editor: Karen Rigden
Creative Director: Miranda Snow
Production: Meskerem Berhane

TOP 10

PARENTS KEEP OUT!

Nature

Paul Terry

FIREFLY BOOKS

TOP 10

PARENTS KEEP OUT!

Nature

We live on a mind-boggling planet! In the pages of this book you'll meet flesh-eating plants, rains of frogs and all the most amazing sights nature has to offer. Earth is beautiful but it can be deadly too. Deadly earthquakes, huge tsunamis and fierce volcanoes sometimes kill thousands of people at a time. Read on for the details of the most amazing, terrifying and just plain bizarre phenomena you've ever seen or imagined.

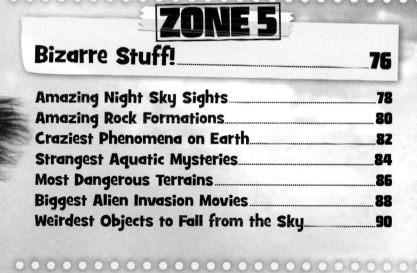

ZONE 1
The Danger Zone...... 8

Deadliest Disasters of All Time...... 10
Deadliest Floods...... 12
Tallest Tsunamis...... 14
Largest Ships Sunk by Nature...... 16
Most Fatal Avalanches...... 18
Deadliest Tornados...... 20
Fastest Cyclones & Hurricanes...... 22
Biggest Volcanic Eruptions...... 24
Biggest Earthquakes...... 26
Most Destructive Hailstorms...... 28
Biggest Disaster Movies...... 30

ZONE 2
Extreme Plants...... 32

Most Carnivorous Plants...... 34
Most Beautiful Plants...... 36
Tallest Trees...... 38
Oldest Trees Alive Today...... 40
Plants With Incredible Uses...... 42
Amazing Healing Plants...... 44

ZONE 3
Amazing Planet...... 46

Biggest Countries (Land Mass)...... 48
Largest Oceans & Seas...... 50
Longest Coastlines...... 52
Longest Mountain Ranges...... 54
Largest Cave Systems...... 56
Highest Waterfalls...... 58
Deepest Lakes...... 60
Largest Craters...... 62

ZONE 4
Extreme Conditions...... 64

Coldest Places...... 66
Hottest Places...... 68
Coolest Weather-reading Tech...... 70
Strangest Weather Events...... 72
Highest Points on Earth...... 74

ZONE 5
Bizarre Stuff!...... 76

Amazing Night Sky Sights...... 78
Amazing Rock Formations...... 80
Craziest Phenomena on Earth...... 82
Strangest Aquatic Mysteries...... 84
Most Dangerous Terrains...... 86
Biggest Alien Invasion Movies...... 88
Weirdest Objects to Fall from the Sky...... 90

MEET...
TEAM T-10

Before you dive into this fact-packed adventure, say hello to the super team who are ready and waiting to guide you through the amazing info zones.

MAY-TRIX

T-10 FILE

This technology-loving 10-year-old girl is the eldest of Team T-10. May-Trix has hundreds of gadgets and gizmos that she uses to scan her surroundings for exciting data. From analyzing animals' sizes and special abilities, to understanding robotics and space exploration, May-Trix adores it all.

APOLLO

T-10 FILE

There are the *Guardians of the Galaxy*, then there's the Keeper of the Comics... And that's Apollo! This 8-year-old boy is an amazing comic book artist, and knows everything there is to know about superheroes, movies, computer games, TV shows and cartoons. He's into sport and outer space, too.

SHAUN VERT

When it comes to extreme sports, fast vehicles, computer games and slammin' metal and rock music, 9-year-old Shaun is your guy! He doesn't go anywhere without his headphones, and he loves cool buildings (he designs skate parks, too). His cybernetic artificial arm allows him to do gravity-defying skateboard tricks.

QUANTUM

Quantum is a very special 7-year-old. Her best friend is her cyborg fish Cy-Go, and her quantum-powered goldfish bowl means she can travel through time and space to learn about the past, the future and the furthest reaches of the universe! This pair love to relax with a movie as well.

ZONE 1
The Danger Zone!

Be warned. Mother Nature is in a pretty bad mood in this zone...

Because even Mother Nature can turn nasty, here are ten events that caused the most casualties.

> A WILDFIRE IN WISCONSIN IN 1871 WAS SO FEROCIOUS AN ESTIMATED 1,200-2,500 PEOPLE DIED.

the lowdown...

Volcanic Eruption

Iceland's Lakagígar volcano spat out 3.35 mi.³ (14 km³) of lava and deadly gases for an insane period of eight months! As most of the island's livestock was killed, a huge number of people also died of hunger.

	TYPE	LOCATION	YEAR	FATALITIES
1	**Volcanic eruption**	**Iceland**	**1783**	**6 MILLION***
2	**Flood**	China	1931	**2.5-3.7 MILLION**
3	**Earthquake**	Shaanxi, China	1556	**820,000-830,000***
4	**Cyclone**	Bangladesh (formerly East Pakistan)	1970	**500,000**
5	**Tsunami**	Several countries	2004	**230,000-310,000**
6	**Heatwave**	Europe	2003	**70,000**
7	**Avalanche**	Peru	1970	**20,000**
8	**Storm**	Venezuela	1999	**15,100**
9	**Blizzard**	Iran	1972	**4,000**
=	**Lightning**	Greece	1856	**4,000**

*Estimated

EPIC FACT

In 1989, a deadly tornado tore through Daultipur, Salturia (Bangladesh), causing 1,300 residents to lose their lives.

IN ANCIENT GREECE, PEOPLE THOUGHT VOLCANIC ERUPTIONS WERE A SIGN THAT THE GODS WERE ANGRY WITH THEM.

STORM

Known as the Vargas Tragedy, rains and flooding struck Vargas State, Venezuela, for three days (December 14-16, 1999). Ten percent of the state's population were killed.

Avalanche

This devastating, icy landslide was caused by the Great Peruvian Earthquake on May 31, 1970, off Peru's coast. The 45-second quake caused an avalanche to smother the towns of Ranrahirca and Yungay.

TOP 10 Deadliest Floods

Earthquakes often cause tsunamis to devastate coastlines, and extreme weather can swamp riverbanks. Floods always leave destruction in their wake.

	RIVER/COUNTRY	YEAR	FATALITIES
1	China	1931	2.5 - 3.7 MILLION
2	Yangtze River & Yellow River (China)	1887	900,000 - 2 MILLION
3	Huang River, Huang He (China)	1938	500,000 - 700,000
4	Indian Ocean Tsunami (several countries)	2004	230,000 - 310,000
5	Banqiao Dam Failure/Typhoon Nina (China)	1975	231,000
6	Yangtze River floods (China)	1935	145,000
7	Messina Earthquake & Tsunami (Italy)	1908	123,000
8	St. Felix's Flood (Netherlands)	1530	100,000+
9	Hanoi & Red River Delta floods (N. Vietnam)	1971	100,000
=	Lisbon Earthquake & Tsunami	1755	100,000

EPIC FACT

One the most effective flood control systems in the world is in the Netherlands.

BANQIAO DAM FAILURE

In 1975, Typhoon Nina led to the collapse of this and 61 other dams in this region of China. As well as the hundreds of thousands who died in the floods, 11 million people had their homes destroyed. As a comparison, that's 2 million more than the current population of London, England.

Indian Ocean Tsunami

Many tsunamis were a part of this 2004 disaster. Waves reached 100 ft. (30 m) high and a staggering 14 countries were affected. Indonesia suffered the most damage and fatalities, with India, Sri Lanka, and Thailand each devastated too.

#3 EARTHQUAKE

The 2004 Indian Ocean Earthquake (which led to the tsunamis) is the third strongest earthquake officially recorded.

LONDON'S RIVER THAMES BARRIER HAS BEEN BEEN CLOSED 174 TIMES FOR FLOOD PREVENTION SINCE IT WAS FINISHED IN 1982.

MOST FLOODED COUNTRIES

NUMBER OF PEOPLE FLOODED (millions)

8.5
8.0
7.5
7.0
6.5
6.0
5.5
5.0
4.5
4.0
3.5
3.0
2.5
2.0
1.5
1.0
0.5

U.S.

HONG KONG

NETHERLANDS

TANZANIA

INDIA

ITALY

UK

UNITED KINGDOM-BASED FLOOD CONTROL INTERNATIONAL CREATED AND SET UP THE BIGGEST FLOOD DEFENSE SYSTEMS ON EARTH.

TOP 10 Tallest Tsunamis

Japanese for "harbour wave," "tsunami" may sound like a poetic word, but it can spell devastation and flooding on a massive scale.

	LOCATION	YEAR	HEIGHT OF TSUNAMI (M)	(FT.)
1	Lituta Bay, Alaska	1958	524	1,179
2	Spirit Lake, Washington	1980	260	853
3	Vajont Dam, Italy	1963	250	820
4	Mount Unzen, Kyushu, Japan	1792	100	328
5	Ishigaki & Miyakojima islands, Japan	1771	79.9	262
6	Lisbon, Portugal	1755	20.1	66
7	Messina, Italy	1908	12.2	40
8	Hoei, Japan	1707	9.8	32
9	Meiji-Sanriku, Japan	1896	9.1	30
10	Haiti	2010	3.1	10

SIZE 'EM UP

Here's a visual guide to how these three tsunamis rank against each other...

ALASKA
1958
HEIGHT: 1,179 ft.
(524 m)

WASHINGTON
1980
HEIGHT: 853 ft.
(260 m)

KYUSHU, JAPAN
1792
HEIGHT:
328 ft. (100 m)

ALASKA

This 1958 event was classified as a megatsunami. 1,179 ft. (524 m) waves were caused by a quake that measured 8.0 on the Richter scale.

EPIC FACT

How tall is this number one? Well, the One World Trade Center is 1,776 ft. (541 m) tall!

Haiti

Before this tsunami in 2010, it had been more than 200 years since Haiti had suffered the effects of a big earthquake. This most recent one had a lengthy reach too. Tsunami waves hit shorelines about 60 mi. (100 km) from Port-au-Prince (the epicenter of the quake).

the lowdown...

THE FIRST OFFICIALLY RECORDED TSUNAMI WAS NEARLY 2,500 YEARS AGO IN ANCIENT GREECE.

TEAM T-10 REPORT

Ancient Waves

A long, long time ago, tsunamis would've reached the heights you see in sci-fi movies. For example, when an asteroid impact caused the Chicxulub crater in Yucatán (in southeastern Mexico) over 60 million years ago, it would've created a megatsunami 3 mi. (5 km) tall!

TOP 10 Largest Ships Sunk By Nature

Smart engineers and designers have come up with some amazing sea-faring craft over the centuries. However, even the biggest and strongest ship is no match for the might of Mother Nature...

SIZE 'EM UP

Here's a comparison of sizes between the ships that sank 100 years apart from each other...

COSTA CONCORDIA
LENGTH:
951 ft. (290 m)

RMS TITANIC
LENGTH:
971 ft. (296 m)

IF YOU'RE INTERESTED IN FINDING OUT MORE ABOUT THE RMS TITANIC, AVATAR DIRECTOR JAMES CAMERON MADE A 2003 DOCUMENTARY IN 3D ABOUT ITS WRECKAGE CALLED GHOSTS OF THE ABYSS.

the lowdown...

RMS Titanic

A total of 1,514 people died when *RMS Titanic* sank, just 2 hours and 40 minutes after it struck an iceberg. The ship left Southampton, England on April 15, 1912, bound for New York City. That was its maiden voyage.

	SHIP	YEAR SUNK	HOW IT SUNK	WEIGHT (T)
1	SS Atlantic Express	1979	Tanker collision during storm	293,000
2	Costa Concordia	2012	Ran aground on rocks	114,000
3	MV Derbyshire	1980	Sank in tropical storm	92,000
4	RMS Titanic	1912	Iceberg collision	46,000
5	Andrea Doria Liner	1956	Hit another ship in fog	30,000
6	MV Princess of the Stars	2008	Capsized during a typhoon	24,000
7	SS Edmund Fitzgerald	1975	Storm and high waves	16,000
8	RMS Republic	1909	Hit another ship in fog	15,000
9	RMS Empress of Ireland	1914	Hit another ship in fog	14,000
10	MS al-Salam Boccaccio	2006	Capsized in heavy storm	5,600

ALSO, TITANIC, JAMES CAMERON'S 1997 MOVIE ABOUT THE RMS TITANIC DISASTER TOOK $2,186,772,302 AT THE BOX OFFICE WORLDWIDE.

ANDREA DORIA LINER

When *SS Andrea Doria* struck another ship, *Stockholm*, on July 25, 1956, 51 people were killed by the impact. The tragedy of this incident is that both ships saw each other on radar, and did try to avoid each other. Sadly, a fault with *Stockholm*'s radar data led to neither ship steering out of harm's way.

EPIC FACT

The cost of getting the *Costa Concordia* back to Genoa to be scrapped, plus the work required to repair Gilgio island, is over $2 billion!

TOP 10 Most Fatal Avalanches

Don't be fooled by video game scenes of heroes snowboarding to escape an avalanche. The truth is deadlier and far more dangerous...

	LOCATION	EVENT	YEAR	FATALITIES
1	Peru	Huascarán avalanche (caused by Ancash earthquake)	1970	20,000
2	Peru	Huascarán avalanche	1962	4,000
3	Austria, Switzerland	649 avalanches (the "Winter of Terror")	1951	265
4	Pakistan	Siachen Glacier avalanche	2012	201*
5	Afghanistan	Salang avalanches (minimum of 36 avalanches)	2010	172
6	Russia	Kolka-Karmadon rock ice slide	2002	125
7	Pakistan	Kohistan avalanche	2010	102
8	U.S.	Wellington, Washington avalanche	1910	96
9	Canada	Frank Slide (buried part of a mining town)	1903	90
10	Afghanistan	Badakshan avalanches (Badakhshan)	2012	50

*incl. 145 presumed

THE FRENCH ALPS' MONT BLANC REGION IS A VERY DANGEROUS PLACE TO CLIMB AND EXPLORE. AVALANCHES CAN MOVE AT UP TO 80 MPH (130 KM/H)!

the lowdown...

Huascarán avalanche

The Ancash earthquake of 1970 cracked the Nevado Huascarán mountain, unleashing an avalanche of ice and rock on the people below. Only 92 survived and the town of Yungay was buried.

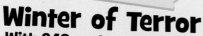

Winter of Terror

With 649 avalanches in this two-year period, it's amazing that only 265 people died. A total of 135 victims were in Austria, and 13 died in one hour when six avalanches struck Andermatt (Switzerland).

SIACHEN GLACIER AVALANCHE

This avalanche struck a Pakistani military base on April 7, 2012. Soldiers and civilians were trapped under 70 ft. (21 m) of icy debris. One hundred and fifty soldiers spent days rescuing as many as they could.

EPIC FACT

The Winter of Terror buried more than 40,000 people under snow.

YOU MAY ALSO KNOW AVALANCHES BY THE WORD "SNOW-SLIDE," AS THIS IS EXACTLY WHAT THEY ARE — FAST-MOVING FLOWS OF SNOW DOWN A SLOPE.

SNOW NETS, BARRIERS AND SNOW DEFLECTION STRUCTURES ARE JUST SOME OF THE THINGS OFTEN BUILT IN PLACES WHERE AVALANCHES ARE A POSSIBILITY.

TOP 10 Deadliest Tornadoes

CGI (Computer-Generated Imagery) in movies may make these twisting funnels of fast-moving air an exciting thing to watch on screen, but in reality, tornadoes are terrifying acts of nature.

	LOCATION	COUNTRY	YEAR	FATALITIES
1	Daultipur & Salturia	Bangladesh	1989	1,300
2	East Pakistan	(now Bangladesh)	1969	923
3	Missouri, Illinois, Indiana	U.S.	1925	695
4	Manikganj, Singair & Nawabganj	Bangladesh	1973	681
5	Valletta's Great Habour	Malta	1551	600
6	Magura & Narail	Bangladesh	1964	500
=	Sicily	Italy	1851	500
=	Madaripur, Shibchar	Bangladesh	1984	500
9	Belyanitsky, Ivanovo, Balino	Russia	1984	400
10	Natchez, Mississippi	U.S.	1840	317

EPIC FACT

Weather satellites positioned high above our planet send us key information. They help us prepare for incoming tornadoes and other deadly forces of nature. The first ever was the U.S.'s Vanguard 2, launched Feb 17, 1959.

Daultipur & Salturia

This is the deadliest tornado in Bangladesh's history. As well as the 1,300 fatalities, a further 12,000 were injured and 80,000 lost their homes to the wrath of the twister. The areas of Manikganj and Saturia were completely destroyed.

TEAM T-10 REPORT

STORM CHASERS RACE IN CARS TO SEE TWISTERS (TRYING TO STAY AT A SAFE DISTANCE)!

Tornadoes

There are lots of different ways to classify how dangerous a tornado is. The Enhanced Fujita Scale was unveiled by the U.S. National Weather Service in 2007. It ranks tornadoes from EF0 for weak twisters up to EF5 for the strongest.

TOP 10 Fastest Cyclones, Hurricares & Typhoons

Tornadoes are not the only air-based form of weather gone wacky. Check out these other kinds of storms, which can reach speeds that would impress even superhero The Flash.

	NAME	YEARS	AFFECTED AREAS	HIGHEST SPEED (KM/H)	(MPH)
1	Cyclone Zoe	2002-03	Solomon Islands, Fiji, Vanuatu, Rotuma	350	217.5
2	Cyclone Inigo	2003	Indonesia, Australia	335	208.2
=	Typhoon Violet	1961	Pacific Ocean	335	208.2
4	Super Typhoon Ida	1958	Japan	325	202
5	Super Typhoon Opal	1964	Kosrae, Chuuk, Philippines	315	195.7
=	Super Typhoon Kit	1967	Japan	315	195.7
=	Typhoon Joan	1959	Taiwan, China	315	195.7
=	Super Typhoon Sally	1964	Philippines, China	315	195.7
9	Typhoon Tip	1979	Guam, Japan	305	189.5
10	Cyclone Glenda	2006	Australia	300	186.4

EPIC FACT

Cyclonic storms also occur on other planets, including the chilly Neptune.

SIZE 'EM UP

It's cyclone speed versus super-fast car...

CYCLONE ZOE
SPEED:
217.5 mph (350 km/h)

BUGATTI VEYRON
(WORLD'S FASTEST PRODUCTION CAR)
SPEED:
267.8 mph (431 km/h)

Cyclone Zoe

Even though 1,700 people who live on the islands were affected by the cyclone, amazingly no one died. For a week after Zoe struck, though, many residents had to survive without much-needed outside aid. Coconut milk became an essential source of food and liquid.

CYCLONE INIGO

This cyclone, along with Gwenda in 1999, is equally the worst to strike this area of the planet. Some areas of Indonesia suffered as much as 9 in. (228 mm) of rainfall in just 24 hours!

THE COST OF STORMS IS HUGE. CYCLONE INIGO LED TO NEARLY $6 MILLION IN DAMAGE REPAIR.

Biggest 10 Volcanic Eruptions

Centuries ago, gods were blamed for these rock formations exploding and spewing deadly lava. Here are the most powerful eruptions ever.

The Tropics

This mysterious eruption is still being investigated, as scientists haven't been able to pinpoint the exact location/volcano that caused it. One of the candidates is El Chichón in Mexico. Humans thought it was dormant until it erupted in 1982!

... IN 2004, ARCHEOLOGISTS UNEARTHED POTS FROM THE 1815 EVENT.

MOUNT TAMBORA'S IS THE MOST POWERFUL ERUPTION EVER RECORDED...

EPIC FACT

Located on the island of Sumbawa in Indonesia, and still very much active, Mount Tambora is a beast of a volcano. When it exploded in April 1815, the sound could be heard over 1,200 mi. (1,930 km) away.

	NAME	LOCATION	YEAR	AMOUNT OF VOLCANIC DISCHARGE (CUBIC KM)	(CUBIC MI.)
1	Unnamed	The Tropics	1258	200-800	48-192
2	Mount Tambora	Lesser Sunda Islands (Indonesia)	1815	150	36
3	Unnamed	New Hebrides (Vanuatu)	1452-53	36-96	8.6-23
4	Kolumbo	Santorini (Greece)	1650	60	14.4
5	Huaynaputina	Peru	1600	30	7.2
=	Long Island (Papua New Guinea)	New Guinea	1660	30	7.2
7	Krakatoa	Indonesia	1883	21	5
=	Quilotoa	Ecuador	1280	21	5
9	Santa Maria	Guatamala	1902	20	4.8
10	Pinatubo	Luzon (Philippines)	1991	6-16	1.4-3.8

PLINIAN ERUPTIONS

These describe eruptions that are similar to Mount Vesuvius' that Pliny the Younger saw in AD 79 at the Gulf of Naples.

the lowdown...

Krakatoa

A 1933 educational short film called Krakatoa won the 1934 Academy Award for Best Short Subject (Novelty). In 2006, the BBC made a drama about the 1883 eruption called *Krakatoa: The Last Days*.

THOSE CRACKS THAT LAVA OOZES OUT OF ARE CALLED FISSURE VENTS. STAND WELL BACK!

Biggest Earthquakes

Another scary part of living on Planet Earth is that its crust can move, causing devastation in many regions around the world.

	LOCATION	DATE	MAGNITUDE (RICHTER SCALE)
1	Valdivia (Chile)	MAY 22, 1960	9.5
2	Alaska, U.S.	MAR. 27, 1964	9.2
3	Sumatra, Indonesia	DEC. 26, 2004	9.1-9.3
4	Tohoku region, Japan	MAR. 11, 2011	9.0
=	Kamchatka, Russia	NOV. 4, 1952	9.0
6	Sumatra, Indonesia	NOV. 25, 1833	8.8-9.2*
7	Ecuador, Columbia	JAN. 31, 1906	8.8
=	Maule, Chile	FEB. 27, 2010	8.8
=	Arica, Chile	SEP. 16, 1615	8.8*
10	Krakatoa, Indonesia	AUG. 26, 1883	8.75

*Estimated

ALASKA

The four-minute-long quake was felt across an unbelievable 501,900 mi.² (1.3 milion km²) from Alaska to areas of Canada and Washington.

TSUNAMI WAVES AS HIGH AS 82 FT. (25 M) WERE CAUSED BY THE VALDIVIA EARTHQUAKE.

VALDIVIA

This is the most powerful earthquake ever recorded. It caused a tsunami to strike the coasts of the Aleutian Islands, Chile, Hawaii, Japan, the Philippines, New Zealand and Australia. The Chilean city of Valdivia suffered the worst damage.

EPIC FACT

Although the total fatalities is unknown, between 2,000 and 6,000 people died as a result of the Valdivia earthquake's effects.

EARTHQUAKETRACK.COM IS AN EXCELLENT WEBSITE THAT TRACKS QUAKE ACTIVITY.

SEISMOMETER

The Greek "seismós" means "shake/quake." Scottish geologist David Milne-Home came up with "seismometer" as the name for fellow Scot and physicist James David Forbes' device that measured ground vibrations.

the **lowdown...**

Arica

In Arica, an area of Tarapaca in Chile, there are quakes almost daily! In 2014 alone there were nearly 300 quakes of varying strength.

TOP 10 Most Destructive Hailstorms

When snow creates a winter wonderland, that can be fun, but when lumps of hard ice start crashing down from the skies? Time to take cover.

	LOCATION	YEAR	DAMAGE (US $)
1	St. Louis, Missouri	2001	2 BILLION
2	Dallas & Fort Worth, Texas	2012	2 BILLION
3	Dallas & Fort Worth, Texas	1995	1.1 BILLION
4	Oklahoma City, Oklahoma	2010	1 BILLION
5	Denver, Colorado	2009	770 MILLION
6	Denver, Colorado	1990	625 MILLION
7	Calgary, Alberta	1991	600 MILLION
=	Wichita, Kansas	1992	600 MILLION
9	Chicago, Illinois	2000	572 MILLION
10	Calgary, Alberta	2010	400 MILLION

ALMOST EVERY BUILDING IN ST. LOUIS SUFFERED HAIL DAMAGE, WITH NEARLY 200,000 INSURANCE CLAIMS MADE!

the lowdown...

St. Louis, Missouri

This horrific hailstorm remains the costliest in the history of the U.S. The blanket of fast winds and deadly hailstones was a staggering 245 mi. (395 km) long and 22 mi. (35 km) across.

Dallas & Fort Worth, Texas

May 5-6, 1995, saw the Tarrant and Fort Worth areas of Dallas, Texas pummeled by hailstones as big as softballs! Thirteen people died and around 100 were injured by the storm.

TEAM T-10 REPORT

Major Damage!

Common injuries include broken bones and severe cuts and bruises — after all, these are fist-sized lumps of ice traveling with storm winds of around 70 mph (120 km/h)! Large hailstones also destroy cars and roofs.

EPIC FACT

South Dakota saw the biggest hailstones ever. In July 2010, some fell that were 8 in. (20 cm) wide.

TOP 10 Biggest Disaster Movies.

Special effects makers love to smash things up on the big screen, and in natural disaster movies, they REALLY go to town, with destruction pushed to the maximum.

	MOVIE	TYPE OF DISASTER	YEAR	BOX OFFICE ($ WORLDWIDE)
1	2012	A natural apocalypse	2009	769,679,473
2	Armageddon	Giant asteroid on course for Earth	1998	553,709,788
3	The Day After Tomorrow	Global warming causes a new ice age	2004	544,272,402
4	Twister	Tornadoes	1996	494,471,524
5	Deep Impact	Comet hits planet Earth	1998	349,464,664
6	The Perfect Storm	A huge wave	2000	328,718,434
7	Waterworld	Polar caps melt, covering Earth in water	1995	264,218,220
8	Poseidon	Giant wave capsizes cruise liner	2006	181,674,817
9	Dante's Peak	Volcanic eruption in Columbia	1997	178,127,760
10	The Impossible	2004 Tsunami that devastated Thailand	2012	172,419,882

EPIC FACT

Some tsunami effects in *The Impossible* were made in a large water tank with miniature sets.

BOX OFFICE

2012
$769,679,473

THE PERFECT STORM
$328,718,434

Each icon represents $50 million

2012

German moviemaker Roland Emmerich is known for his love of disaster movies. As well as end of the world epic *2012*, he made *The Day After Tomorrow* (2004), "aliens attack Earth" movie *Independence Day* (1996) and *Godzilla* (1998).

THE PERFECT STORM

Unlike most of the movies here, *The Perfect Storm* is actually based on real-life events. Sebastian Junger wrote an account of the crew of the *Andrea Gail* fishing boat that got caught in a terrifying storm in 1991. Junger's book was published 1997. Director Wolfgang Petersen also made this top 10's number 8, *Poseidon*.

> GOT AN IDEA FOR A NATURAL DISASTER MOVIE THAT HASN'T BEEN MADE YET? TIME TO WRITE YOUR FIRST SCREENPLAY!

the lowdown...

Armageddon

This was the biggest box office hit of 1998, which was quite a year for "the Earth may be destroyed" movies. Ten weeks after *Armageddon* was released, *Deep Impact* came out. Both dealt with an asteroid on a course to smash our planet.

ZONE 2
Extreme Plants

If you thought vegetation was bland, think again.... These are power plants!

EPIC FACT

The Venus Flytrap is an evil genius of a plant. Its brightly colored insides attract its prey, which then accidentally tread on "trip wire" hairs. This makes the trap close, and then digestion begins!

THIS MEAT-EATER WAS AN INSPIRATION FOR THE SINGING, MAN-EATING ALIEN PLANT AUDREY II IN THE LITTLE SHOP OF HORRORS STAGE SHOW AND MOVIE!

the *lowdown*...

Green Pitcher Plant

Cool and carnivorous it may be, but the Green Pitcher sadly needed to be covered by the U.S.'s Endangered Species Act. The biggest threat to them is us. Too many companies are selling them to plant collectors.

TOP 10 Most Carnivorous Plants

Groot from *Guardians of the Galaxy* may be a lovable giant, but some of the plants you'll find in the real world have a taste for blood!

	NAME	TRAP TYPE	TRAPS & EATS
1	Giant Malaysian Pitcher Plants	Pitfall/cup trap	Rats, mice, lizards, frogs, insects
2	Cobra Lily	Cobralike pitcher trap	Flies, ants, beetles, crawling insects
3	Common Bladderwort	Aquatic hair-trigger bladder traps	Baby fish, tadpoles, round worms
4	Waterwheel Plant	Aquatic hair-trigger bristle trap	Water fleas, tadpoles
5	West Australian Pitcher Plant	Pitfall/cup trap	Ants, small insects
6	Green Pitcher Plant	Pitfall/cup trap	Wasps and other small insects
7	Venus Flytrap	Hair-trigger jaws/trap	Small insects and arachnids
8	Cape Sundew	Sticky tentacles	Small insects and arachnids
9	Rainbow Plant	Sticky barbs	Small insects
10	Yellow Butterwort	Sticky leaves	Flies and small insects

SCIENTISTS BELIEVE THE FIRST "SNAP-TRAP" PLANTS EVOLVED 65 MILLION YEARS AGO!

Cape Sundew

Originating from South Africa, this is a plant with insect-eating tentacles! When its victim is caught by the gluey prongs, the arm slowly curls inward, trapping its dinner inside the rolled-up squidlike arm.

TOP 10 Most Beautiful Plants

Some can look like creepy things out of Sleepy Hollow, but other plants are like stunning, glorious works of art.

NAME

#	Name
1	White Lotus
2	Bird of Paradise
3	Passion Flower
4	Rose
5	Cherry Blossom
6	Plumeria
7	Dahlia
8	Magnolia
9	Oriental Poppy
10	Gazania

Bird Of Paradise

This super striking flower comes from South Africa, and it's easy to see how it got its name. And it's no delicate little flower — it grows to more than 6 ft. (2 m) tall. Being such a stunning plant, it's no surprise it's been adopted as the official flower of Los Angeles, California, and is often used in design work to represent paradise.

THE BIRD OF PARADISE IS OFTEN MISTAKEN FOR A BANANA PLANT.

MAGNOLIA

In 1703, French botanist (plant scientist) Charles Plumier named a type of flower on the Caribbean island of Martinique a "magnolia" after another French botanist he knew, Pierre Magnol.

White Lotus

Also known as the Tiger Lotus, this is the national flower of Egypt. Thousands of years ago in Ancient Egyptian times, the White Lotus was actually worshipped. It was believed to represent creation and was also used to make perfume.

the lowdown...

MANY BUDDHISTS BELIEVE THAT EVERY SOUL EMERGES FROM A LOTUS FLOWER.

EPIC FACT

The White Lotus was also the name of an ancient group seeking truth, beauty and philosophy.

TOP 10

Tallest Trees

How big is the tallest person you know? Multiply that person's height by 50 and you'll start to get close to the size of these titanic species.

	TYPE	LOCATION	MAXIMUM KNOWN HEIGHT (M)	(FT.)
1	Coast Redwood	California	115.72	379.65
2	Douglas Spruce	Oregon	99.76	327.3
3	Victorian Ash	Tasmania, Australia	99.6	327
4	Sitka Spruce	California	96.7	317
5	Giant Sequoia	California	95.8	314
6	Tasmanian Blue Gum	Tasmania, Australia	90.7	298
7	Manna Gum	Tasmania, Australia	89	292
8	Yellow Meranti	Sabah, Borneo	88.3	290
9	Alpine Ash	Tasmania, Australia	87.9	288
10	Klinki Pine	Morobe Province, Papua New Guinea	70+	229.7

GIANT SEQUOIA

These magnificent trees are only found in the Sierra Nevada area of California. The oldest is 3,500 year old! Via their pinecones, they can release up to 400,000 seeds every year. Young trees start to shed seeds from 12 years of age.

EPIC FACT

The Stagg (a Giant Sequoia in Sierra Nevada's Alder Creek Grove) has a diameter of 22.9 ft. (7.05 m) just above the ground. General Sherman (in Tulare County, California) has a volume of 52,508 ft.^{3} (1,486.9 m^3).

Sitka Spruce

If you love music, you should be very thankful for the Sitka Spruce tree. Its wood is amazing at conducting sound, so a high percentage of pianos, guitars, violins and many other musical instruments are made from this tree. Its cool name comes from the people of Sitka, Alaska.

Coast Redwood

The tallest tree in the world is Hyperion, a Coast Redwood in Redwood National and State Parks in Northern California. Naturalists Chris Atkins and Michael Taylor discovered Hyperion in 2006.

CHANDELIER TREE
Height: 315ft Diameter: 21ft
Maximum Age: 2400yrs
DRIVE THRU TREE, Leggett, CA

IN DRIVE-THRU TREE PARK IN LEGGETT, CALIFORNIA YOU CAN DO... WELL, GUESS WHAT!

IF YOU WANT TO VISIT METHUSELAH, YOU'LL HAVE A HARD TIME FINDING IT. ITS PRECISE LOCATION WITHIN THE INYO NATIONAL FOREST IS KEPT A SECRET TO PROTECT THE TREE.

the **lowdown**...

Methuselah
California

This magnificent tree lives in the Methuselah Grove area of an ancient bristlecone pine forest in California. This forest is around 2,800 ft. (2,987 m) above sea level. It's part of Inyo County's White Mountains.

EPIC FACT

If you visit Hampton Court Park in London, England you can visit another tree called the Methuselah Oak. It's 750 years old.

TOP 10 Oldest Trees Alive Today

The oldest ever human lived for 122 years, but these trees of the world make that length of time seem like the blink of an eye.

	NAME	SPECIES	LOCATION	VERIFIED AGE (YEARS)
1	(Unnamed)	Great Basin Bristlecone Pine	California	**5,062**
2	Methuselah	Great Basin Bristlecone Pine	California	**4,845**
3	(Unnamed)	Patagonian Cypress	Los Lagos, Chile	**3,642**
4	The President	Giant Sequoia	Nevada	**3,200**
5	CB-90-11	Rocky Mountain Bristlecone Pine	Colorado	**2,455**
6	Jaya Sri Maha Bodhi	Sacred Fig	North Central Province, Sri Lanka	**2,217**
7	Bennett Juniper	Western Juniper	Nevada	**2,200**
8	SHP 7	Foxtail Pine	Nevada	**2,110**
9	(Unnamed)	Subalpine Larch	Alberta	**1,939**
10	CRE 175	Rocky Mountain Juniper	New Mexico	**1,889**

FIND OUT MORE ABOUT ANCIENT TREES AT YOUR LOCAL NATURAL HISTORY MUSEUM.

Jaya Sri Maha Bodhi

Bodhi is a special word in Buddhism. It means "to understand the true nature of things," and you may have heard it described as "enlightenment." You'll find bodhi trees close to Buddhist monasteries.

TOP 10 Plants With Incredible Uses

The natural world is an amazing place that offers us an endless bounty of useful things. Look at how amazing plants can be...

	PLANT	USES
1	**Bamboo**	Housing, tools, rafts
2	Skunk Bush	Natural deodorant
3	Cane Reed	Musical instruments
4	Giant Reed	Water pipes
5	Musk Mallow	Natural insecticide
6	Oil Palm	Biodiesel (fuel made from plants)
7	Hyacinth Orchid	Ink
8	Cotton Plant	Clothing
9	Goat Willow	Faux leather
10	Greasewood	Basket-weaving

the **lowdown...**

Hyacinth Orchid

Not only is this awesome orchid used to give certain inks a glossy quality, it's also been used in China to treat ailments for over 1,500 years! Everything from nosebleeds to cuts and burns get the Hyacinth Orchid approach.

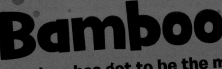

Bamboo

Bamboo has got to be the most versatile plant ever. Beyond the uses we've listed in the Top 10, bamboo can also be transformed into musical instruments, clothes, martial arts weaponry, hunting bows, fishing rods and even snowboards and bicycles!

MUSK MALLOW

Enjoy trying new foods? Well, you can munch on musk mallow seeds. You'll often see its flowers and leaves served up as part of a wild salad in restaurants too.

TAKE A LOOK AROUND YOUR HOME AND YOUR SCHOOL... HOW MANY DIFFERENT USES FOR PLANTS CAN YOU FIND? CHALLENGE YOUR FRIENDS TO FIND THE MOST!

EPIC FACT

Bamboo is officially the fastest growing plant, with some species growing up to 35.8 in. (91 cm) in one day! There are more than 1,000 different kinds of bamboo, with tropical locations seeing them grow to 130 ft. (39.6 m) high.

TOP 10 Amazing Healing Plants

As well as being pretty to look at, many plants can actually help to relieve mental and physical health conditions.

	PLANT	MEDICINAL QUALITY
1	St. John's Wort	Helps treat mental health conditions like depression
2	Peppermint	Good for congestion, headaches and digestion
3	Blackberry	Leaves can ease diarrhea
4	Lady Ferns	Its juices help ease pain of stinging nettles
5	Witch Hazel	Helps treats skin conditions like eczema
6	Catnip	Relieves headaches, stomach pains and colds
7	Dill	Good for indigestion
8	Honeysuckle	Its flowers, brewed, ease fever and flu symptoms
9	Snapdragon	Helps treat burns
10	Strawberry	Its leaves, when brewed, help sore throats

STRAWBERRY

Over 5 million tons of strawberries are grown and sold each year, with 1.5 million from U.S. alone.

Snapdragon

These got their fantastic name because their flowers look like a dragon's face. Their oil is sometimes extracted for cooking, plus, a dye can be made from the flower.

the lowdown...

Witch Hazel

The spooky part of this plant's name doesn't have any relation to ghouls and goblins. It comes from the old Middle English (a language used around the 12th-15th centuries), where the word "wiche" meant "bendy."

THE EBERS PAPYRUS, WRITTEN BY THE ANCIENT EGYPTIANS OVER 3,500 YEARS AGO, HAS DETAILED INFO ON ABOUT 850 HEALING PLANTS AND HERBS.

LONDON'S CHELSEA PHYSIC GARDEN, DEDICATED TO HEALING PLANTS, HAS BEEN THERE SINCE 1673!

EPIC FACT

Peppermint has an antiseptic quality and fights germs that can cause bad breath.

PEPPERMINT

This plant is actually a hybrid, which means it's made from two different species. This cross between spearmint and watermint is very popular worldwide as a flavoring and for natural remedies, especially its extracted oil.

ZONE 3

Amazing Planet!

Earth is a world of natural wonders,
so let's get exploring...

U.S.

Across its 50 states, this country is home to over 30 million people! Its vast lands contain 256.646 mi.² (664.709 km²) of water in lakes and rivers. There are also 58 national parks.

the **lowdown...**

The Biggest of Them All

Russia is so large that it makes up more than an eighth of the Earth's inhabited lands. It has 144 million residents, making it the ninth most populated country in the world. Its biggest city, Moscow, is also the capital.

I LOVE EVERYTHING TO DO WITH TIME. RUSSIA AMAZES ME BECAUSE NINE DIFFERENT TIME ZONES EXIST ACROSS THIS MASSIVE COUNTRY!

TOP 10 Biggest Countries (Land Mass)

Planet Earth has a LOT of countries. If you had to guess, which would you say were the largest 10? Find out below.

	COUNTRY	SIZE (SQUARE KM)	(SQUARE MI.)
1	**Russia**	**17,098,242**	**6,601,668**
2	Canada	9,984,670	3,855,100
3	China	9,706,961	3,747,879
4	U.S.	9,629,091	3,705,407
5	Brazil	8,514,877	3,287,612
6	Australia	7,692,024	2,969,907
7	India	3,166,414	1,222,559
8	Argentina	2,780,400	1,073,500
9	Kazakhstan	2,724,900	1,052,100
10	Algeria	2,381,741	919,595

Population Change

Over a hundred years ago, Kazakhstan was home to less than 25,000 people. Now, almost 18 million live there. Almaty is the most populated city in Kazakhstan, home to 1.6 million people.

TOP 10 Largest Oceans & Seas

About 71 percent of our planet's surface is covered with water. It's thought that 50 to 80 percent of life on Earth lives there too!

	NAME	TYPE	SIZE (SQUARE KM)	(SQUARE MI.)
1	Pacific	Ocean	166,266,876	64,196,000
2	Atlantic	Ocean	86,505,602	33,400,000
3	Indian	Ocean	73,555,662	28,400,000
4	Southern	Ocean	52,646,688	20,327,000
5	Arctic	Ocean	13,208,939	5,100,000
6	Philippine	Sea	5,179,976	2,000,000
7	Coral	Sea	4,791,478	1,850,000
8	Arabian	Sea	3,861,672	1,491,000
9	South China	Sea	2,973,306	1,148,000
10	Caribbean	Sea	2,514,878	971,000

Pacific Ocean

The largest ocean in the world is even bigger than you might think. It covers over 30 percent of our planet. That means it takes up more space than ALL of the countries put together.

the lowdown...

Indian Ocean

The Indian Ocean is beautiful, but sea levels are rising fast due to climate change, and some islands could sink under the water in the next few years.

ARCTIC OCEAN

Sea water is famed for being salty, but the Arctic Ocean has the lowest salt levels of all the oceans. Global warming due to pollution is having a devastating effect on the poles of our planet. Experts fear the Arctic could have zero frozen ice by 2040.

CORAL REEFS MAY LOOK LIKE ROCKS, BUT THEY'RE ACTUALLY MADE OF TINY ANIMALS CALLED POLYPS.

TOP 10 Longest Coastlines

Team T-10 loves to visit the seaside – and you could make an awful lot of sandcastles on some of these shores!

	COUNTRY	LENGTH OF COASTLINE	
		(KM)	(MI.)
1	Canada	265,523	164,988
2	United States	133,312	82,836
3	Russia	110,310	68,543
4	Indonesia	95,181	59,143
5	Chile	78,563	48,812
6	Australia	66,530	41,340
7	Norway	53,199	33,056
8	Philippines	33,900	21,064
9	Brazil	33,379	20,741
10	Finland	31,119	19,336

FOSSILS OFTEN SHOW UP IN COASTAL CLIFFS AS THE SEA ERODES THEM.

the lowdown...

Canada

Nearly 36 million people live in this country, which is north of the U.S. You may not know that English and French are both official languages of Canada.

Australia

Western Australia features the longest of the country's coastlines at nearly 8,080 mi. (13,000 km). But as 70 percent of Australia is desert — called the outback — the population is only 23 million.

Brazil

If hanging out on the beach is one of your favorite things to do when you go on vacation, you may want to visit Brazil. Its coastlines feature 2,095 different beaches!

SURFING HAS BEEN PRACTICED FOR THOUSANDS OF YEARS ON COASTLINES AROUND THE WORLD.

EPIC FACT

Canada's name is an Iroquoian word for "settlement."

TOP 10 Longest Mountain Ranges

We're exploring rock regions, but with a twist! Team T-10 have combined mountains above AND below the water's surface.

	RANGE	MOUNTAIN TYPE	LOCATION	LENGTH (KM)	LENGTH (MI.)
1	Mid-Oceanic Ridge	Oceanic	Global	65,000	40,389
2	Mid-Atlantic	Oceanic	Atlantic Ocean	10,000	6,214
3	Andes	Oceanic	South America	7,000	4,350
4	Rockies	Land	North America	4,800	2,983
5	Transantarctic	Land	Antarctica	3,542	2,201
6	Great Diving Range	Land	Australia	3,059	1,901
7	Himalayas	Land	Asia	2,576	1,601
8	Southeast Indian Ridge	Oceanic	Indian Ocean	2,300	1,429
9	Southwest Indian Ridge	Oceanic	Rodriguez Island to Prince Edward Islands	1,931	1,200
10	Pacific-Antarctic Ridge	Oceanic	South Pacific Ocean	1,029	639

EPIC FACT
The name "Himalayas" comes from a Sanskrit word (from Hindu language) which translates as "home of the snow." Seems appropriate!

CHECK YOUR LOCAL MUSEUM TO FIND OUT MORE ABOUT HOW MOUNTAINS ARE FORMED.

GREAT DIVIDING RANGE

The highest point of this epic Australian range is Mount Kosciuszko, which is a cool 7,310 ft. (2,228 m) high. It crosses through three states.

Mid-Oceanic Ridge

Don't be fooled into thinking that this underwater mountain range is a place of peace and cool waters. As many as 20 volcanic eruptions a year occur along its length!

the **lowdown**...

EPIC FACT

Did you know there are plenty of mountain ranges on the moon, too?

The Rockies

The Rockies aren't just amazing mountains to look at (and to Instagram). They're a favorite for skiers, too! But be careful if you're visiting, as they are also home to predators like bears and wolves...

EPIC FACT

The full name of Mammoth Cave, Kentucky, is the Mammoth-Flint Ridge Cave System. Don't expect to find woolly mammoth fossils there, though. Its name just means it's huge.

Beneath Your Feet

There may even be a cave system beneath your feet right now. Look into the history and geology of where you live to find out if there are any nearby caverns where you can go on a guided tour.

the lowdown...

Lechuguilla Cave

If you're a fan of the BBC series *Planet Earth*, you may remember seeing New Mexico's Lechuguilla Cave featured. It has an amazing depth of 1,604 ft. (489 m).

TOP 10 Largest Cave Systems

Batman may have an awesome cave of gadgets and gizmos, but these underground caves are thousands of times larger.

	CAVE NAME	LOCATION	LENGTH (KM)	(MI.)
1	Mammoth Cave	Kentucky	643.7	400
2	Sistema Sac Actun/ Sistema Dos Ojos	Quintana Roo, Mexico	311	193.3
3	Jewel Cave	South Dakota	267.6	166.3
4	Sistema Ox Bel Ha	Quintana Roo, Mexico	244.3	151.8
5	Optymistychna Cave	Korolivka, Ukraine	236	146.6
6	Wind Cave	South Dakota	226.1	140.5
7	Lechuguilla Cave	New Mexico	222.6	138.3
8	Hölloch	Muotathal, Switzerland	200.4	124.5
9	Fisher Ridge Caves	Kentucky	191.7	119.1
10	Gua Air Jernih	Sarawak, Malaysia	189.1	117.5

THE HÔLLOCH CAVE SYSTEM, WHICH IS RICH IN LIMESTONE, WAS FIRST EXPLORED IN 1875.

Angel Falls

American aviator Jimmie Angel's name was given to the falls because he was the first to fly them (on November 18, 1933). He had his ashes scattered over Angel Falls after he died in 1960.

 the **lowdown**...

NEW ZEALAND'S BROWNE FALLS ARE NAMED AFTER LEGENDARY PHOTOGRAPHER VICTOR CARLYLE BROWNE. HE DISCOVERED THEM IN THE 1940S.

Tugela Falls

Tugela Falls is created by the water from the 312-mi. (502 km) long Tugela River, the largest river in South Africa's KwaZulu-Natal Province.

TOP 10 Highest Waterfalls

If you think that a waterfall that's twice as high as the Empire State Building sounds like something from *Star Wars*, think again!

	NAME	LOCATION	HEIGHT (M)	HEIGHT (FT.)
1	Angel Falls	Bolívar State (Venezuela)	979	3,212
2	Tugela Falls	KwaZulu-Natal, South Africa	948	3,110
3	Cataratas las Tres Hermanas	Ayacucho, Peru	914	3,000
4	Olo'upena Falls	Molokai, Hawaii	900	2,953
5	Catarata Yumbilla	Amazonas, Peru	896	2,940
6	Vinnufossen	Møre og Romsdal, Norway	860	2,822
7	Balåifossen	Hordaland, Norway	850	2,788
8	Pu'uka'oku Falls	Molokai, Hawaii	840	2,756
=	James Bruce Falls	British Columbia	840	2,756
10	Browne Falls	South Island, New Zealand	836	2,743

EPIC FACT

Located on the island of Molokai in Hawaii, Pu'uka'oku Falls feature cliffs that rise more than 0.65 mi (1 km) high.

TOP 10 Deepest Lakes

Lakes all over planet Earth are home to stories of monster sightings. Some of them certainly have a lot of room for giant creatures to live in!

	NAME	LOCATION	LENGTH (M)	(FT.)
1	Baikal	Siberia (Russia)	1,637	5,371
2	Tanganyika	Tanzania, Democratic Republic of the Congo, Burundi, Zambia	1,470	4,823
3	Caspian Sea	Iran, Russia, Turkmenistan, Kazakhstan, Azerbaijan	1,025	3,363
4	Vostok	Antarctica	1,000	3,281
5	O'Higgins-San Martin	Chile, Argentina	836	2,743
6	Pinatubo	Philippines	800	2,625
7	Malawi	Mozambique, Tanzania, Malawi	706	2,316
8	Issyk Kul	Kyrgyzstan	668	2,192
9	Great Slave	Canada	614	2,015
10	Crater	Oregon	594	1,949

Tanganyika

This lake has 325 different species of fish, including the awesomely named Tanganyika killifish. It covers a massive 12,703 mi.² (32,900 km²) area.

PINATUBO

You might be surprised to hear that this lake was only formed in 1991. It was created after the eruption of Mount Pinatubo that year.

the **lowdown**...

Baikal

Lake Baikal is frozen from January to May each year. The 395-mi. (636-km) long body of water was home to an ancient Siberian tribe known as the Kurykans, back in the sixth century.

EPIC FACT

Lake Vostok is the biggest lake in the Antarctic, which is home to not 100, not 200, but close to 400 lakes!

IS THE CASPIAN A LAKE OR A SEA? EXPERTS CAN'T DECIDE. IT'S BIG ENOUGH TO BE A SEA, BUT IT'S TOTALLY SURROUNDED BY LAND, LIKE A LAKE.

Largest Craters

When asteroids smashed into our planet millions of years ago, they caused dents in the Earth's surface that we call craters.

	NAME	LOCATION	AGE (MILLIONS OF YEARS)	DIAMETER (KM)	(MI.)
1	Vredefort	Free State, South Africa	2,023	300	186.4
2	Sudbury	Ontario, Canada	1,849	250	155
3	Chicxulub	Yucatán, Mexico	65	170	105
4	Kara	Nenetsia, Russia	70.3	120	75
5	Manicouagan	Québec, Canada	215	100	62
=	Popigai	Siberia, Russia	35.7	100	62
7	Acraman	South Australia	580	85-90	53-55
8	Chesapeake Bay	Virginia, U.S.	35.5	85	53
9	Puchezh-Katunki	Nizhny Novgorod Oblast, Russia	167	85	50
10	Morokweng	Kalahari Desert, South Africa	145	70	43

Manicouagan

Some scientists believe that this crater in Québec could have been struck by more than one asteroid. One of its most stunning features is Lake Manicouagan, which formed a circle of water around the edge of the crater.

ZONE 5: Amazing Planet!

SUDBURY CRATER

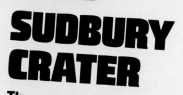

The research carried out by experts at Trinity College Dublin led to the conclusion that the Sudbury Crater, over 9 mi. (14.5 km) deep, had been caused by a comet.

Vredefort

The explosion that created the Vredefort crater in South Africa was so powerful it must have been equal to several nuclear bombs. The crater is also a World Heritage Site, meaning it is protected from commercial development.

the **lowdown...**

AN ASTEROID STRIKING EARTH CAN CAUSE TEMPERATURES OF THOUSANDS OF DEGREES.

EPIC FACT

Australia's Acraman crater was caused by an asteroid striking the Earth 580 million years ago.

ZONE 4

Extreme Conditions!

Pack your warmest coat and also your best sunglasses for this crazy zone...

Snow way

Mohe County is located in Heilongjiang province, the top northeastern region of China. It's so cold it's known as China's "Arctic Village," and winter there lasts for seven months (from October to April).

PHILOSOPHERS IN ANCIENT GREECE (600 BC) WERE RIGHT IN THINKING THERE WERE NORTH AND SOUTH POLES!

EPIC FACT

Mohe County is one of the places you can see the Aurora Borealis. The colored lights swirling in the sky are caused by electrically charged particles in the air.

the lowdown...

South Pole First Place

Explorers have been managing to get close to the South Pole for hundreds of years, but it wasn't until Dec. 14, 1911, that humans reached it. The successful expedition was Norway's Roald Amundsen and his team.

TOP 10 Coldest Places

Team T-10 love playing in the snow, but temperatures that make icicles form on your nose wouldn't tempt us outside to make a snowman!

	LOCATION	DATE	TEMPERATURE (ºC)	TEMPERATURE (ºF)
1	Vostok Station, Antarctica	Jul 21, 1983	-89.2	-128.6
2	Amundsen-Scott South Pole Station (South Pole)	June 23, 1982	-82.8	-117
3	Dome A, East Antarctica	July 2007	-82.5	-116.5
4	Verkhoyansk & Oymyakonm Sakha Republic, Russia	Feb. 6, 1933	-68	-90
5	North Ice, Greenland	Jan. 9, 1954	-66.1	-87
6	Snag, Yukon, Canada	Feb. 3, 1947	-63	-81
7	Prospect Creek, Alaska, U.S.	Jan. 23, 1971	-62	-80
8	Ust-Shchuger, Russia	Dec. 31, 1978	-58.1	-72.6
9	Malgovik, Västerbotten, Sweden	Dec. 13, 1941	-53	-63.4
10	Mohe County, China	Feb. 13, 1969	-52.3	-62.1

TOP 10 Hottest Places

You'll need a lot more than sunglasses and sunblock if you visit any of these places! Check out the crazy-hot temperatures.

	LOCATION	DATE	TEMPERATURE (°C)	(°F)
1	Death Valley, California, U.S.	July 10, 1913	56.7	134
2	Kebili, Tunisia	July 7, 1931	55	131
3	Tirat Zvi, Israel	June 21, 1942	54	129
4	Sulaibya, Kuwait	July 31, 2012	53.6	128.5
5	Kuwait International Airport, Kuwait	Aug. 3, 2011	53.5	128.3
=	Mohenjo-daro, Sindh, Pakistan	May 26, 2010	53.5	128.3
7	Nasiriyah, Ali Air Base, Iraq	Aug. 3, 2011	53	127.4
8	Basra, Iraq	June 14, 2010	52	125.6
=	San Luis Río Colorado, Mexico	July 6, 1966	52	125.6
=	Jeddah, Saudi Arabia	June 22, 2010	52	125.6

FREEZING HOT

If you hate winter, Jeddah's climate would work very well for you. Temperatures can often be 82°F (28°C) on a wintry afternoon! Want to know the coldest it has ever been here? A "chilly" 51.8°F (11.0°C).

EPIC FACT

In the hottest places on Earth, milk stays fresh because the heat kills off bacteria!

Deathly Hot!

The Mojavi desert, in Eastern California, is the location of Death Valley. In 2001, a record 154 days in a row saw temperatures stay above a scorching 100°F (38°C).

the **lowdown**...

KUWAIT HAS ALMOST NO PRECIPITATION FOR THE MONTHS OF OCTOBER, NOVEMBER AND DECEMBER.

ANCIENT HUMANS

Kebili, a town in South Tunisia, has evidence that people have lived in the Tunisian region for over 200,000 years.

HAARP-ANTENNA

Standing for High-frequency Active Auroral Research Program, HAARP's research is focused on surveillance and radiowaves in the ionosphere of our planet. This refers to the area 37-370 mi. (60-600 km) above the Earth's surface.

the lowdown...

ONE OF THE FIRST SUNDIALS, WHICH TELLS THE TIME OF DAY, WAS CREATED IN EGYPT OVER 4,500 YEARS AGO.

EPIC FACT

Sci-fi fans, check this out. Some people believe that the true purpose of HAARP is mind control!

Sling psychrometer

Humidity is all about how much moisture there is in the air, and the sling psychrometer was designed to measure it.

70

TOP 10 Coolest Weather-reading Tech

How do we get to hear such amazingly accurate weather reports? It's thanks to super devices like these.

#	TECHNOLOGY	MEASURES
1	**HAARP** (High-frequency Active Auroral Research Program)	**Various/ionosphere activity**
2	**Polar-orbiting Satellite**	Various
3	**Geostationary Satellite**	Various (from a "fixed point" in orbit)
4	**Lightning Detector**	Lightning
5	**Doppler Weather Radar**	Locate and calculate rain, snow and hail
6	**Sling Psychrometer**	Relative humidity
7	**Anemometer**	Wind speed
8	**Hygrometer**	Humidity
9	**Barometer**	Air pressure
10	**Thermometer**	Air temperature

Lightning Detector

The first ever lightning detector was invented by Russian scientist Alexander Stepanovich Popov in 1894. He even has an asteroid name after him, "3074 Popov."

THE STUDY OF THE EARTH'S ATMOSPHERE IS CALLED METEOROLOGY.

TOP 10 Strangest Weather Events

Forget the basics of wind, rain, snow and sunshine. We're about to find out about some of the weirdest kinds of weather ever.

1	**Moonbow**
2	Sun Ghost
3	Aurora Borealis
4	Belt of Venus
5	Mammatus Clouds
6	St. Elmo's Fire
7	Diamond Dust
8	Green Ray
9	Light Pillars
10	Supercells

Weird Green

These are stages of a setting sun. If you look closely at the top of each sun, you can see a green shape. Green rays can happen during sunset or sunrise. The brief glimpse of green happens because of the way light separates into different colors in Earth's atmosphere.

MOON PHENOMENA

Notice how sometimes the moon is so bright you can see the world around you? Moonbows are made by the moon's light - especially when it's super bright - refracting off water droplets in the air, in the same way that sunlight creates rainbows.

the **lowdown**...

EPIC FACT

If sunlight passes through a cloud that contains ice crystals, you may see a circular halo effect called a sun ghost.

HAVE YOU SEEN ANY OF THESE AMAZING WEATHER EVENTS? ASK YOUR FRIENDS AND FAMILY IF THEY HAVE TOO!

Sci-Fi Sky

It may look like a scene from *The Avengers*, but this occurs naturally in nature! Charged particles from the sun enter the Earth's atmosphere and hit particles of gas. The amazing colors occur due to the different types of gas.

TOP 10 Highest Points on Earth

Explorers who have a head for heights love going to the top of mountain ranges that are over 5 mi. (8 km) high.

	PLACE	PART OF MOUNTAIN RANGE	HEIGHT (M)	HEIGHT (FT.)
1	Mount Everest/Sagarmatha Chomolungma	Mahalangur Himalaya	8,848	29,029
2	K2/Qogir/ Godwin Austen	Baltoro Karakoram	8,611	28,251
3	Kangchenjunga	Kangchenjunga Himalaya	8,586	28,169
4	Lhotse	Mahalangur Himalaya	8,516	27,940
5	Makalu	Mahalangur Himalaya	8,485	27,838
6	Cho Oyu	Mahalangur Himalaya	8,188	26,864
7	Dhaulagiri I	Dhaulagiri Himalaya	8,167	26,795
8	Manaslu	Manaslu Himalaya	8,163	26,781
9	Nanga Parbat	Nanga Parbat Himalaya	8,126	26,660
10	Annapurna I	Annapurna Himalaya	8,091	26,545

Mt. Manaslu

Birdwatchers can have the time of their lives on this mountain in Nepal. About 110 different species of birds live in the area, including the majestic Golden Eagle.

Mount Everest

Mount Everest is the highest mountain on the planet. Its first official height measurement (which was 26 ft. [8 m] less than its actual agreed height now) was recorded and published in 1856.

WHAT IS THE TALLEST BUILDING OR PLACE WHERE YOU LIVE? WHAT'S THE TALLEST IN YOUR WHOLE COUNTRY?

KANGCHENJUNGA

Like many mountains, this place has its own legendary monster. People on a trip in 1925 reported seeing a Yeti-type creature that has since become known as the Kangchenjunga Demon.

EPIC FACT

Seventeen-year-old Indian Arjun Vajpai became the youngest climber of Lhotse in 2011.

ZONE 5

Bizarre Stuff!

There are a lot of weird and wonderful things on and from Earth, so let's investigate...

Andromeda Galaxy

How far away would you guess this galaxy is? How does 2.5 million light years sound? It's true! Scientists are also interested in the 14 mini galaxies that are around it, called dwarf galaxies.

WHAT HAVE YOU SEEN IN THE NIGHT SKY WITH YOUR NAKED EYES?

the lowdown...

Lagoon Nebula

This amazing pink swirl is an interstellar cloud. This means it is a collection of gases and dust particles that exist in another galaxy, far away from our solar system.

TOP 10 Amazing Night sky Sights

From down here on Earth, we can see some incredible things above us, especially at night-time with a telescope or a pair of binoculars.

1	**The Lagoon Nebula**
2	The Andromeda Galaxy
3	Hercules Cluster
4	Orion
5	The Frying Pan
6	The Crab Nebula
7	Jupiter
8	The Pleiades
9	Pole Star
10	The Moon

EPIC FACT

Orion is also the name of an MPCV (Multi-Purpose Crew Vehicle) that's being developed to help us explore the further reaches of space... maybe even including the mission to Mars!

Pole Star

The Pole Star is one of the brightest things you'll see in the sky at night. It has helped captains navigate their way across the oceans for centuries.

Amazing Rock Formations

These miracles of nature rock harder than any guitar band! Check out the these weird and wonderful natural features.

	NAME	LOCATION
1	Uluru	Northern Territory, Australia
2	Giant's Causeway	County Antrim, Northern Ireland
3	Ergaki Hanging Rock	Central Siberia, Russia
4	Fairy Chimney	Pasabag Valley, Turkey
5	Ko Tapu	Khao Phing Kan, Thailand
6	Devil's Tower	Black Hills, Crook County, Wyoming, U.S.
7	Queen's Head	Yehlia Geopark, Taiwan
8	Balancing Rock	Garden of the Gods, Colorado, U.S.
9	Reed Flute Cave	Guilin, Guangxi, China
10	Wave Rock	Hyden, Western Australia

ROCK HISTORY

Uluru is sacred to Australia's Aborigines. Studies have revealed that humans have lived in the region for at least 10,000 years. Humans aside, 21 different species of animal live near and around the ancient rock.

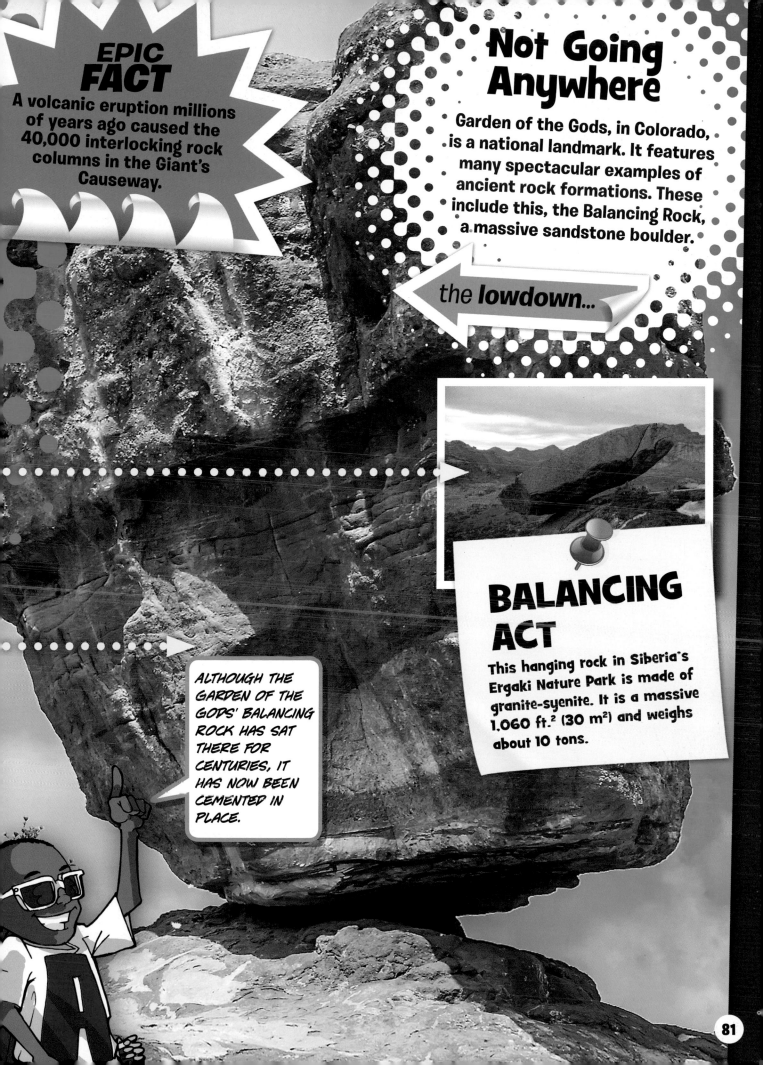

EPIC FACT

A volcanic eruption millions of years ago caused the 40,000 interlocking rock columns in the Giant's Causeway.

Not Going Anywhere

Garden of the Gods, in Colorado, is a national landmark. It features many spectacular examples of ancient rock formations. These include this, the Balancing Rock, a massive sandstone boulder.

the **lowdown...**

BALANCING ACT

This hanging rock in Siberia's Ergaki Nature Park is made of granite-syenite. It is a massive 1,060 ft.² (30 m²) and weighs about 10 tons.

ALTHOUGH THE GARDEN OF THE GODS' BALANCING ROCK HAS SAT THERE FOR CENTURIES, IT HAS NOW BEEN CEMENTED IN PLACE.

Deadly Water

The sinkhole that appeared in Mulberry, Florida was very dangerous, but not because of its size or depth but because mud and dirt got into the local water supply, contaminating it and causing $6 million worth of damage.

EERIE EXPLOSION

The blast incident at Tunguska, Russia, is so mysterious that more than 1,000 official documents have been published about it. Everything from a government experiment to a black hole has been blamed for it.

EPIC FACT

Sinkholes can reach amazing sizes... Up to 2,000 ft. (600 m) wide! They are caused naturally by surface cave-ins, but can also happen when mines or pipes collapse.

TOP 10 Craziest Phenomena on Earth

Unexplained events like these could have come straight out of a superhero comic. But these are all 100 percent real!

	EVENT	LOCATION	YEAR	DETAILS
1	The Tunguska Blast	Tunguska, Siberia	1908	A mysterious explosion 1,000 times more powerful than the Hiroshima bomb.
2	The Great Smog	London, England	1952	Dense fog and coal-burning (to keep warm) led to 12,000 breathing-related deaths.
3	Fire Devil	Kantō, Japan	1923	The Great Kantō earthquake created a fiery vertex that killed almost 40,000 people.
4	Killer Hailstorms	Gopalganj, Bangladesh	1986	Two-pound hailstones killed nearly 100 people.
5	The 10 Year Storm	U.S.	1930-1940	Massive dust storms hit the U.S. over a period of 10 years.
6	Mass Deaths	Lake Nyos, Cameroon	1986	Thousands were killed by what scientists think was volcanic gas from Lake Nyos.
7	Florida Sinkholes	Florida, U.S.	1994	This naturally occuring sinkhole in Florida caused a gigantic load of toxic mud to sink into the ground!
8	Elephant Stampede	Chandka Forest, India	1972	Drought and a heat wave caused elephants to stampede, killing 24 people.
9	Year without a Summer	U.S., Canada, Europe	1816	Low temperatures, frost and snowfall persisted through the summer months
10	Tri-State Tornado	Missouri, Illinois, Indiana, U.S.	1925	This tornado wrecked parts of three states.

Fire Devil

These devastating swirls of air have a center that is on fire, caused by intense winds and rising heat.

TOP 10 Strangest Aquatic Mysteries

Some ocean mysteries date back hundreds of years. These are Team T-10's favorites.

	MYSTERY	DETAILS
1	**Bermuda Triangle**	Why do boats and planes keep disappearing between three coastal points off Florida, Puerto Rico and Bermuda
2	Lost City Of Atlantis	Is there really a massive island that sank to the bottom of the Atlantic Ocean?
3	The Mary Celeste	Discovered abandoned in 1872, with its sails up, and the crew's possessions intact. What happened?
4	Underwater voices	In 1997 and 1999, what made the creepy sounds that were caught on microphones?
5	UFO on ocean bed	Do researcher Peter Lindberg's sonar recordings prove a UFO is on the sea bed between Finland and Sweden?
6	Alaskan sea monster	In 2009, fisherman Kelly Nash captured footage that looks like a sea serpent swimming in Nushagak Bay.
7	Ghost ships	Are spectral, crew-less vessels just a trick of the light?
8	Mermaids	In 1998, did diver Jeff Leach capture footage of a real mermaid off the coast of Hawaii?
9	The Montauk Monster	What was the odd-looking dead animal found on the coast of New York in 2008?
10	The Philadelphia Experiment	Were the military involved with experiments to warp space-time back in 1943?

Ghost Ship

This eerie phenomena may sound crazy, but there have been dozens of regular sightings since the 1700s. One of the most famous is the Lady Lovibond, which is said to be seen off the southeast coast of England every 50 years.

The Bizarre Stuff!

BERMUDA TRIANGLE

This area is between Florida, San Juan in Puerto Rico, and the island of Bermuda. Some people blame the disappearance of planes and ships inside the area on aliens!

the lowdown...

EPIC FACT

Many countries including the U.S., Canada, Scotland, Italy, and China have reports of lake monsters.

WHICH OF THESE MYSTERIES EXCITES YOU THE MOST? INVESTIGATE YOUR FAVORITE FURTHER!

MONTAUK MONSTER

This carcass washed up on a beach near Montauk, New York. Some people who have examined it claim that it is a decomposed raccoon. However, others are unconvinced, and suggest it could be the body of an as yet unknown species. How it died is not clear.

TOP 10 Most Dangerous Terrains

"Watch your step" is the understatement of the century when it comes to surviving a trek through these crazy places.

	PLACE	LOCATION
1	**Skippers Canyon**	**Queenstown, New Zealan**
2	**Mount Huashan**	Shaanxi, China
3	**Yungas Road (The Death Road)**	Yungas, Bolivia
4	**Tenaya Canyon**	Yosemite National Park, California
5	**Annapurna Mountain**	Himilayas, Nepal
6	**Baintha Brakk (The Ogre)**	Gilgit–Baltistan, Pakistan
7	**Grimsel Pass**	Alps, Switzerland
8	**El Caminito del Rey (King's Little Path)**	Málaga, Spain
9	**Guoliang Tunnel**	Taihang Mountains, Henan, China
10	**Sichuan-Tibet Highway**	China-Nepal Border

Skippers Canyon

This gorge in New Zealand is 13.7 mi. (22 km) long. Tourists flock to Skippers Road, the main access point, to experience the amazing views of the gorge. The road is very dangerous, with drops of over 2,000 ft. (610 m).

TIBET HIGHWAY

This 1,499-mi. (2,412-km) long road takes brave travelers through 14 mountains. These are up to 16,000 ft. (5,000 m) high. The full length of the highway provides hot sun and snow at different points.

the lowdown...

PAKISTAN'S THE OGRE IS A 23,900-FT. (2,285-M) HIGH RUGGED MOUNTAIN.

Death Road

There are no crash barriers on Yungas Road, otherwise known as the Death Road. With drops of 1,000 ft. (300 m), hundreds of people are thought to die there each year.

TOP 10 Biggest Alien Invasion Movies

These are the movies that made the most money out of aliens attacking and destroying Earth.

EPIC FACT

The Avengers is the third most successful movie of all time, just behind *Titanic* and *Avatar*.

Smash-Up

The director who brought aliens to try to destroy Earth in *Independence Day*, Roland Emmerich, also made a movie in 1998 where a big beast smashes New York City. *Godzilla!*

Avengers

the lowdown...

When the Chitauri attack New York City they bring massive space eel-type creatures called Leviathans. These were never in the Marvel *Avengers* comics and were actually created by director Joss Whedon and writer Zak Penn.

	MOVIE	YEAR OF THE RELEASE	BOX OFFICE ($ WORLDWIDE)
1	The Avengers	2012	1,518,594,910
2	Transformers: Dark of the Moon	2011	1,123,794,079
3	Transformers: Age of Extinction	2014	1,087,404,499
4	Transformers: Revenge of the Fallen	2009	836,303,693
5	Independence Day	1996	817,400,891
6	Transformers	2007	709,709,780
7	Man of Steel	2013	668,045,518
8	Thor: The Dark World	2013	644,783,140
9	Men In Black 3	2012	624,026,776
10	War of the Worlds	2005	591,745,540

Falling Frogs

Frogs and toads have been reported to fall out of the sky all over the world throughout history. This includes Illinois in 1883, Serbia in 2005 and China in 2008.

the lowdown...

THERE ARE WRITTEN RECORDS OF ANIMALS FALLING FROM THE SKY BACK IN THE FIRST CENTURY AD!

Huge Metal Sphere

This was thought to be a piece of a satellite, but was it part of a UFO? At 3 ft. (1 m) across and a weight of 110 lb. (50 kg), the villagers of Riacho dos Poços thought a plane had crashed.

EPIC FACT

Severe weather like tornadoes can cause animals and objects to be whipped up, carried, and then dropped miles later.

TOP 10 Weirdest Objects to Fall from the Sky

Next time you're stuck out in heavy hail, rain, or snow, spare a thought for the people who had these things falling on their heads...

	OBJECT	LOCATION	DATE
1	Frogs	Naphlion in Southern Greece	May 1981
2	Huge metal sphere	Brazil	Feb. 23, 2012
3	Spiders	Argentina	Apr. 6, 2007
4	Frogspawn	Port-Au-Prince, Haiti	May 5, 1786
5	Cone-shaped Metallic object	Novosibirsk, Russia.	Mar. 20, 2012
6	Fish	Great Yarmouth, UK	Aug. 6, 2000
7	Jelly rain	Pentlands, Scotland	Oct. 17, 2008
8	Unknown whale-sized object	Litchfield, Connecticut	Apr. 12, 2012
9	Golf balls	Punta Gorda	Sep. 1, 1969
10	100 starlings	Somerset, England	Mar. 2010

FREAKISH FEATHERS

Scientific experts cannot explain why dozens of starlings fell out of the sky and struck the ground of a single garden in Somerset, England. Mass bird deaths have been linked to UFO sightings.

TIME TO GET INTERACTIVE!

It's time to blast off from planet Earth and investigate something else awesome. See how well you and your friends know our world with this quick quiz...

Questions from... ZONE 1

1 Can you put these natural disasters in the order of how deadly they were?

A: Peru's 1970 avalanche

B: Iceland's 1783 volcanic eruption

C: China's 1931 flood

2 True or false: the 1958 tsunami in Alaska was 172 ft. (52.4 m) high?

TRUE ☐ FALSE ☐

3 Which of this movies about natural disasters made the most money at the box office?

A: Waterworld ☐

B: The Impossible ☐

C: Twister ☐

Questions from... ZONE 2

1 Can you name this carnivorous plant?

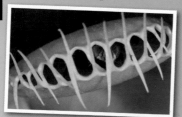

2 True or false?

A: Hyperion isn't the tallest tree in the world?

TRUE ☐ FALSE ☐

B: The Douglas Spruce lives in Africa.

TRUE ☐ FALSE ☐

C: Tasmanian Blue Gum is the name of a real tree.

TRUE ☐ FALSE ☐

3 What is the fastest growing plant?

Questions from... ZONE 3

1 Can you name 2 countries that are in the top 3 biggest?

2 What is the largest ocean?

3 Which person led to the waterfall Angel Falls getting its name?

Questions from... ZONE 4

1 Can you remember the hottest place on Earth?

2 Where do Green Rays appear?

A: Underwater
B: Above the sun
C: Under trees

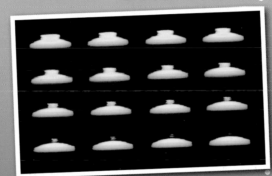

3 True or false: a moonbow is a real thing that happens in nature.

TRUE   FALSE

Questions from... ZONE 5

1 Where is Uluru located?

2 Which famous blast in 1908 remains unexplained?

3 Can you put these "aliens attacking Earth" movies in the order of their box office success?

A: Men In Black 3
B: The Avengers
C: War Of The Worlds

ANSWERS:

ZONE 5
1: Australia
2: Tunguska
3: B, A, C

ZONE 4
1: Death Valley, California
2: B
3: TRUE

ZONE 3
1: Russia, Canada, China
2: Pacific
3: Jimmie Angel (American aviator)

ZONE 2
1: Venus Flytrap
2: A - FALSE, B - FALSE, C - TRUE
3: Bamboo

ZONE 1
1: B, C, A
2: FALSE: it was 524 m high
3: C

THAT WAS AWESOME! HOPE YOU ENJOYED THE RIDE.
WE SURE DID.
TEAM T-10

Also available:

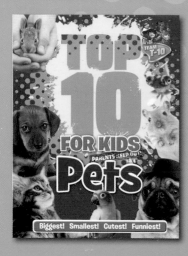

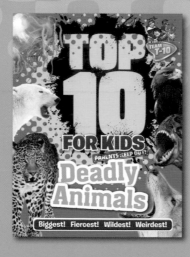

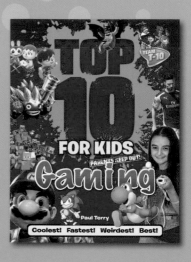

PICTURE CREDITS

The publishers would like to acknowledge the following sources in the book:

4. Jiji Press/AFP/Getty Images (trees), Cultura Science/Jason Persoff Stormdoctor/Getty Images (tornado), 8. Shutterstock.com (volcano), Nicholas Kamm/AFP/Getty Images (destroyed houses), Jiji Press/AFP/Getty Images (trees), AF Archive/Alamy (boat in storm), 10. Shutterstock.com, 11. Blickwinkel/Alamy, 12-13. Richard Dirscherl/Getty Images, 13 Pornchai Kittiwongsakul/AFP/Getty Images, 14-15. Richard Dirscherl/Getty Images, 15. Nicholas Kamm/AFP/Getty Images, 16. Bob Thomas/Popperfoto/Getty Images, 16-17. Shutterstock.com, 18-19. Ed Darack/Getty Images, 19. Shutterstock.com, 20. Erik Simonsen/Getty Images, 20-21. Cultura Science/Jason Persoff Stormdoctor/Getty Images, 21. InterNetwork Media/Getty Images, 22-23. Jiji Press/AFP/Getty Images, 23. Stocktrek Image, Inc./Alamy, 24-25. Sebastian Crespo Photography/Getty Images, 25. Arlan Naeg/AFP/Getty Images, 26-27. NigelSpiers/Shutterstock.com, 27. Nicholas Kamm/AFP/Getty Images (destruction), Getty Images (Seismometer), 29. Tetra Images/Johannes Kroemer/Getty Images (road), Ales Veluscek/Getty Images (hailstones), 30-31. Deltev van Ravenswaay/Getty Images, 31. AF Archive/Getty Images, 32-33. Shutterstock.com, 32. Nikada/Getty Images (stilt houses), Shutterstock.com (Venus flytrap), 33. Shutterstock.com (white flower & Pitcher plant), 34. Shutterstock.com (Pitcher plant & flytrap), 35. Andy Nixon/Getty Images, 36-37. Shutterstock.com 38. Rafal Dubiel/Getty Images (tree), 38-39. Istockphoto.com, 39. Sarah Leen/Getty Images, 40-41. Shutterstock.com, 42. Datacraft Co Ltd/Getty Images, 42-43. Istockphoto.com, 43. Mark Hamblin/Getty Images (flower), Shutterstock.com (pesticide), Nikada/Getty Images (stilt house), 44-45. Shutterstock.com, 46. Shutterstock.com (Brazil & Antarctica), Sakis Papadopoulos/Getty Images (Maldives), 46-47. Shutterstock.com (waterfall), Matthieu Paley/Getty Images (frozen lake), 48-49. Planet Observer/Universal Images Group via Getty Images, 48. Shutterstock.com, 49. Shutterstock.com, 50. Jason Edwards/Getty Images, 51. Sakis Papadopoulos/Getty Images (Maldives), 51. Shutterstock.com (Antarctica), 52-53. Ascent Xmedia, 53. Getty Images (Gold Coast), Shutterstock.com (Rio), 54-55. Dr Ken Macdonald/Science Photo Library, 55. Stephanie Jackson/Australian Landscapes/Alamy (forest), 55. Shutterstock.com (lake), 56. Michael Nichols/Getty Images, 56-57. Stephen Alvarez/Getty Images, 58-59. Shutterstock.com, 60-61. Matthieu Paley/Getty Images (frozen lake), 60. Robert Harding Picture Library/Alamy, 61. Shutterstock.com, 62. NASA/Expedition 12, 62-63. Planet Observer/Universal Images Group via Getty Images, 63. Planet Observer/Science Photo Library, 64. Shutterstock.com (mountains), Noppawat Tom Charoensinphon/Getty Images (Northern Lights), Jim Goldstein/Alamy (rainbow), Shutterstock.com (winter road), 64-65. Shutterstock.com (Everest), 66. Shutterstock.com, 66-67. NSF/Josh Landis/Antarctic Photo Library, U.S. Antarctic Program, 68. Still Works/Getty Images, 68-69. Shutterstock.com, 69. Godong/Getty Images, 70. Randall Benton/Sacramento Bee/MCT via Getty Images (Sling Psychrometer), Science Photo Library/Alamy (HAARP), 71. Shutterstock.com, 72. Brocken Inaglory, 72-73. Jim Goldstein/Alamy, 73. Noppawat Tom Charoensinphon/Getty Images, 74-75. Shutterstock.com, 76. Walt Disney/Everett/Rex, (The Avengers), Debbie Egan-Chin/NY Daily News Archive via Getty Images (sinkhole), Sovfoto/UIG via Getty Images (highway), 76-77 (Garden of the Gods), 76-77. Samuel D. Barricklow/Getty Images (thunderstorm), 78. Adam Evans, 78-79. ESO/VPHAS+ team, 79. Stan Honda/AFP/Getty Images, 80. Nicole Duplaix/Getty Images, 80-81. Shutterstock.com, 81. Stardancer, 82-83. Debbie Egan-Chin/NY Daily News Archive via Getty Images, 83. The Asahi Shimbun via Getty Images, 84. AF Archive/Alamy (ghost ship), 84-85. Victor Habbick Visions/Getty Images, 85. Jenna Hewitt, 86. Ben Davies/LightRocket via Getty Images, 86-87. DeAgostini/Getty Images, 87. Sovfoto/UIG via Getty Images (highway), 88. Moviestore Collection/Alamy, 88-89. Walt Disney/Everett/Rex, 90-91. Shutterstock.com, 92. Shutterstock.com (mountains), Noppawat Tom Charoensinphon/Getty Images (Northern Lights, Jim Goldstein/Alamy (rainbow), Sovfoto/UIG via Getty Images (highway), 93. Walt Disney/Everett/Rex (The Avengers), Shutterstock.com (road), Debbie Egan-Chin/NY Daily News Archive via Getty Images (sinkhole).

· ·

Top 10 For Kids! Nature Produced by WILDPIXEL LTD

Writer & Researcher: Paul Terry

Picture Research: SpookyFish

Illustrations: Huw J

Project Editor: Anna Bowles

· ·

Special thanks to...

Ian Turp & Marc Glanville at Getty Images

David Martill, Palaeobiologist

Box office information courtesy of The Internet Movie Database (http://www.imdb.com).
Used with permission.

· ·

The publishers gratefully acknowledge the permission granted to reproduce the copyright material in this book. Every effort has been made to trace copyright holders and to obtain their permission for the use of copyright material. The publisher apologizes for any errors or omissions in the above list and would be grateful if notified of any corrections that should be incorporated in future reprints or editions of this book.